ST. AUGUSTINE'S GHOSTS

SEASIDE PUBLISHING

ST. AUGUSTINE'S
GHOSTS
THE HISTORY BEHIND
THE HAUNTINGS

KAREN HARVEY

Seaside Publishing

Gainesville · Tallahassee · Tampa · Boca Raton

Pensacola · Orlando · Miami · Jacksonville · Ft. Myers · Sarasota

For information about permission to reproduce selections from this book, write to
Permissions, 15 Northwest 15th Street, Gainesville, FL, 32611-2079.

Library of Congress Control Number: 2018940938

ISBN 978-0-942084-43-6

SEASIDE PUBLISHING

Seaside Publishing is a division of the University Press of Florida.

For a complete list of Seaside books, please contact us

Seaside Publishing

15 Northwest 15th Street

Gainesville, FL 32611-2079

1-352-392-6867

1-800-226-3822

orders@upress.ufl.edu

www.seasidepublishing.com

CONTENTS

ST. AUGUSTINE'S GHOSTS

INTRODUCTION

GHOSTS, SPIRITS, POLTERGEISTS—whatever label you wish to apply—have a place in American civilization, whether an individual acknowledges them by a name or not. Legends and stories about supernatural occurrences are retold endlessly with believers and nonbelievers perpetuating them over generations. The question is why these stories are so important to us and why we feel compelled to resurrect them every day.

Author Colin Dickey wrote about the interaction of ghosts and history in *Ghostland: An American History in Haunted Places*. He said, "Ghost stories in many ways are a way for us to approach our own history."[1]

Fabricated ghost stories are as fragile as dandelion blooms in a breeze. The stories that persevere are stories with relevance to a person and his or her family, or tales that connect some-one to a particular building or geographic area.

In St. Augustine, Florida, the oldest continuously occupied settlement in the continental United States, visitors come to see and hear about local ghosts as they absorb the intricate history of the former colonial village. Many guests choose to immerse themselves in the city's ghost stories by staying in bed-and-breakfast inns that have a reputation of hauntings. The stories abound, and integral to the stories are St. Augustine's Spanish and Minorcan roots.

St. Augustine's history includes Spanish lore and the unique history of the Minorcan culture. The Spanish arrived on Florida's shores in 1565 and stayed until 1821 with the exception of the twenty-year occupation of the British from 1763 to 1784.

The British Period is significant for the introduction of indentured servants to Florida. The term "Minorcan" refers collectively to a group of willing men and women brought to Florida by Dr. Andrew Turnbull. Single men and families were imported from the island of Minorca, one of three Balearic Islands in the Mediterranean Sea, which at the time was a British possession. People from Italy, Greece, and Corsica were included in the mass importation. This was the largest single group of European settlers to immigrate as a unit to the New World.

These men and women worked an indigo plantation in New Smyrna until a group of approximately seven hundred marched to St. Augustine in 1777 for sanctuary. They remained in the city when Florida was returned to Spain in 1784 and were firmly established in St. Augustine when the peninsula became American territory in 1821. They remain the core group of America's oldest city.

The Menorcan Cultural Society was founded in the 1980s to preserve and promote the heritage and culture of the Menorcans who left their Mediterranean homeland to make a new life in the New World. The society chose to use the spelling of "Menorcan" with an "e" rather than the earlier use of "Minorcan" with an "i." They are the only Menorcan society in the United States and enjoy a worldwide membership.

All the ghost stories throughout this book—whether of Spanish or Minorcan origin—are part of St. Augustine's history. Many of the stories take place on St. George Street, one of the oldest streets in the United States. The Plaza de la Constitución, the oldest extant landmark in the United States, also features several ghost stories. Originally used as the center of town in 1572–73, it became the official plaza in 1598 by a Spanish government decree requiring all colonial positions to construct a central location according to specific measurements and design.

The streets around the rectangular plaza extend from the corners in the directions of north and south, east and west. Visitors and residents walk the streets daily, and the town is full at night with ghost tours. The sightseers have kept nightlife alive; before the tours, St. Augustine shut down at the end of a workday. Now the streets are filled with folks eager to hear the stories and the city's history. It should be understood that some tours tell stories that are historically correct; others tell stories that are fabricated. Explaining history through storytelling has been done for centuries; here in St. Augustine we try to capture history through our ghost stories.

1

COLONIAL
SPANISH
TALES

1565-1821

THE LAUNDRY LADY

The pedestrian-friendly portion of St. George Street running from the City Gate to the plaza is the nucleus of a multitude of ghost tours in St. Augustine. It is appropriate that tours are provided in this location, since it was once the heart of Spanish colonial St. Augustine. Some stories are centuries-old legends, but some have occurred since the tours began.

This is a story of what one man witnessed in the 1990s.

Garrett, a young actor, and his friends were working in the Spanish Inn, a tavern on St. George Street located in a portion of town known to have been populated by the colonial Spanish. Five tavern employees were cleaning up after the restaurant closed, and Garrett was responsible for disposing of a bag of garbage. He simply needed to cross the pedestrian-only corridor and pass through the courtyard on the other side in order to reach a dumpster. It was a mundane and unthreatening task. That night, however, it was not a routine job.

Garrett walked across the street, turned into the courtyard of the Spanish Bakery, and was surprised to see a woman in a long Spanish colonial skirt, white shift, and laced-up peasant bodice hanging laundry over a bush. He noticed garments and white sheets spread across the courtyard picnic tables.

Seeing actors and tour guides in period clothing is quite normal in downtown St. Augustine, and the appearance of a woman dressed in that manner was not at all disturbing to

Garrett. He stopped to say "hello" to the woman, but she didn't respond to his greeting.

Thinking perhaps she was deaf, Garrett stepped closer so as not to frighten her.

Then he suddenly felt a chill. He shivered and looked at the lady. Her long skirt was blowing in the breeze and hanging fabric was flapping over the bushes. Garrett knew there was no wind stirring the air. Certain by then he was seeing a ghost, Garrett dropped his sack of garbage and backed away.

Running to the tavern, he summoned his friends. Three of them retuned with him to the courtyard. They turned the corner. No one was standing by the bush.

Garrett looked around and spotted the colonial figure in the back of the yard, silently hanging up more laundry. He pointed her out to his friends, who clearly saw the woman by the fence.

"That's no ghost, you jerk," one friend commented.

"Prove it," Garrett said.

They went to the figure and tried to get her attention. She never stopped her laundry duties and never acknowledged their presence. Garrett pleaded to his friends to touch her, knowing an earthly being cannot feel a ghost. No one would make physical contact with her.

Finally, the four, in a panic, decided to go back to get a fifth person who had experienced other spiritual activity. The five ran back to the courtyard.

This time no one appeared to them. The courtyard was empty. They walked around searching, peering around walls and investigating darkened corners. She was gone. All the laundry was gone. The only thing left was Garrett's garbage bag, and no one wanted to move it to the dumpster in the back of the courtyard for fear of the lady showing up again.

The tale of the laundry lady is popular in St. Augustine. One tour guide said, "The idea of residual energy and repetitive acts for all eternity seems to fascinate people."[1]

The courtyard of the Spanish Bakery is no longer available for tours. Guides now use the Artisan's Arcade near the St. George Inn when bringing their groups on tours.

The Salcedo Kitchen inside the courtyard is known as the Spanish Bakery and sells homemade breads and soups. It is a reconstruction built in the 1960s about the same time as the historic Salcedo House on the property was reconstructed. Both represent our colonial history and more.

Today, the proprietors lock the gate in the wall surrounding the courtyard. I think I know why.

ELIZABETH: A TEENAGER ROBBED OF HER DIGNITY

The story of Elizabeth Forrester is intriguing. Shuttle trains and trolley drivers say Elizabeth stands at the City Gate, warning people away from the Huguenot Cemetery during the yellow fever epidemic. There may be a ghost at the City Gate, but if it is Elizabeth, the train and trolley guides do not have their facts right.

The truth is far more interesting than the fabricated stories. Elizabeth, also known as Yzabel, was born in 1782. That was the end of the British Period (1763–84) in St. Augustine and the beginning of the Second Spanish Period (1784–1821). She died at age sixteen and is entombed in the Tolomato Cemetery on Cordova Street as the oldest burial in that sacred plot of ground.

According to the inscription on her tomb, she fought hard against her illness. Although the exact nature of her sickness is unknown, her experience seems similar to teenagers fighting cancer today. The inscription reads that she bore illness "With true Christian fortitude." These words follow, saying, "She fought [sic] a better world amidst the tears of her disconfolate [sic] relatives."

Elizabeth was a young girl with strength. Her family names indicate she was of both Spanish and English heritage. A page in the Tolomato Cemetery books notes that Elizabeth's parents were Dona Dionsisia Hull and Geraldo Forrester. Don Geraldo's parents were Don Patrico and Dona Brigida (probably Brigita).

Here we have the documented evidence of a story that should be retold. Grave robbers stole her clothes in 1809. According to Elizabeth Gessner, president of the Tolomato Cemetery Preservation Society, this was not unusual. Textiles were a valued commodity, and robbing graves for fabric happened frequently.[2]

Elizabeth may stand at the City Gate. I can't say. I do know she did not die in the yellow fever epidemic of 1821 and would not be warning people to stay away because of illness.

The beauty of this tale is that a young girl is remembered through these stories. I can picture a sixteen-year-old courageously fighting to live. Then, to have her clothing stolen after she died, that's enough to make anyone roll over in his or her grave.

I hope Elizabeth's story will continue to live on. She should be remembered for enduring illness in life and humiliation in death.

LITTLE BOY JAMES

The Brownie Scouts fidgeted at the gate of the Tolomato Cemetery in the evening darkness. They knew no one could enter the cemetery, and they were willing to wait outside to hear the ghost stories. The tale teller, Ted, stood before the wire gate, holding his lantern high while relating legends of spirits haunting the historic grounds.

Orbs can be seen in this photo of the tree where James has been sitting on the branches. The Tolomato Cemetery is a popular location for the ghost tours, and the story of James is fascinating more because so many people see him rather than for his historical significance. Photo courtesy of Tour St. Augustine.

The first Brownie to see the little boy did not question his appearance. She walked up to Ted at the gate and reached behind him for the white rose petal the five-year-old boy handed to her. A second girl followed and accepted a petal from his hands.

Ted continued his storytelling as the third little girl came forward and returned to the back of the group of about twenty. The three girls huddled together near the street bordering the cemetery when suddenly they screamed and started crying.

Ted, concerned for the safety of his group, parted the crowd and approached the girls.

With gulps of breath between sobs, the little girls insisted that a boy had presented them with flower petals and then flew up into one of the large cedar trees in front of them. They opened empty palms and said the rose petals disappeared once the boy had left the ground and landed on a large branch

The tombstone of James clearly states his age. Photo by Karen Harvey.

overhanging the wire fence. He then disappeared into a bright halo of light.

No one in the group that night would forget what happened. James's tombstone reads:

JAMES P.
Son of
E. & A.M. Morgan
DIED
Nov. 28, 1877
(Age) 5 yrs. & 10 days.

James did nothing in his short life of five years to make a mark in history, but he lives on in the hearts of those little girls who saw him and held the white rose petals in their hands. His tombstone is in the front of the Tolomato Cemetery on Cordova Street, visible to all passersby.

The little boy continues to be seen, usually in branches of the tree shading the recently reconstructed fence. He will be remembered as long as tour guides relate his tale. If they stopped speaking of him, would he then be forgotten?

CATALINA RETURNS HOME

Catalina DePorras was a child when the unthinkable happened. Spanish Florida was given to the British in a diplomatic trading maneuver. Despite the attacks of Governor James Moore in 1702 and General James Oglethorpe in 1740, the British never conquered St. Augustine or took control of *La Florida*. However, in 1763 the British, hungry for more land to colonize, occupied Florida by a treaty agreement. Havana had been captured by Great Britain during the Seven Years' War, and Spain wanted it back. In a massive exodus from Florida, every man, woman, and child fled to Cuba, including Spanish citizens, free blacks, and some Native Americans.

Catalina, the youngest in a family of several children, was one of them. Her dream was to live again in the home on the bayfront facing the harbor. She was determined to come back to St. Augustine, and her wish finally came true. Once Florida was reinstated as Spanish territory, Catalina sailed to her homeland to reclaim the house of her parents. Unfortunately, the home was in disrepair, and legal problems prevented her from enjoying it in the last years of her life. She died within a few years of her return to St. Augustine. But she did not leave the house. Her presence is felt in the historic home, usually with appearances in the second-floor ladies' powder room.

Today the house on the bayfront with the address of 46 Avenida Menendez is Harry's Seafood Bar and Grille. It was, at one time, called Catalina's Garden. Her ghost was less active then, and it is suggested she might have liked the name and felt comfortable there.

The house appears on an 1840s sketch of bayfront homes, drawn and engraved by John S. Horton. The stone coquina garden archway remains the entrance to the patio of this popular restaurant.

Several stories are told about Catalina. One observer, Adele Wright, an employee of a bed-and-breakfast with frequent accounts of spiritual activity, remembers when the restaurant was called the Chart House. She was in the women's restroom when she saw the reflection of someone behind her in a colonial-style white dress with long hair. She knew it was Catalina.

On a different occasion, a woman told me she was in the restroom stall when her purse started swinging from side to side. She was so upset she sat down in a wicker chair in the lounge to regain her composure. While there, she felt someone tap her on the shoulder and the chair moved. She thought her luncheon companion had entered, but no one was there.

Employees know Catalina's spirit inhabits the house because they will check the restroom and then return to see tissues strewn about the counter when no one has entered. They also attribute Catalina's presence to the smell of perfume. The aroma is prevalent at unusual times and cannot be attributed to a person.

This author was walking down the street across from the restaurant when a man who had been on a ghost tour with me the previous night told me he had seen Catalina in the window and had captured her image on film. No matter how many times I have walked down that street, I have never seen Catalina in the second-story window, but a photograph documented her face. I would like to see her, but she has not graced me with her presence in the restaurant or at the window.

Her home remains a significant architectural landmark. The style is called St. Augustine Colonial Revival and represents the Spanish and British construction methods. It is two-and-a-half stories with balconies, dormers, and shutters. Although most of the original building burned in a fire in 1887, the current structure is built to look like the house Catalina loved. It remains an outstanding structure on the city's bayfront. Catalina would be proud.

YELLOW ROSES

On South St. George Street, just past the plaza, is a house with history and hauntings. One of the legends that is repeated here was related to me by Eleanor Philips Barnes in the 1980s.

Mrs. Barnes was a genealogical researcher of St. Augustine residents. While producing records for family interests, Mrs. Barnes uncovered facts which enriched our understanding of the heritage of the city. This story is of particular value since it connects several periods of history into one story. It takes place in a house still in existence at 214 St. George Street.

In Mrs. Barnes words:

Brigita Arrendondo was enchanted by the garden in the courtyard of her house on St. George Street. She had frequent conversations among the flowers with the dearly departed spirits of Maria and Antonia Horruytiner (pronounced "Ooo-root-tin-air"). Maria Ruiz was the wife of Don Pedro Horruytiner who had possibly occupied a house on the property in the 1600s. Antonia was her daughter-in-law.

The current house became an issue with Brigita and her husband in 1819 at the time Florida was being transferred from Spanish to American occupation. Fernando Arrendondo wished to return to Cuba, but Brigita loved the house and wanted to stay in St. Augustine. Brigita's husband told her he would keep the house if she would give up her nonsensical dreams of chatting with the mystical women.

One day Brigita was seated on a bench in her lovely garden, amidst her gorgeous roses, dreaming and wishing about going back in history to meet the ladies who had lived there.

As she contemplated her beautiful surroundings, Maria Ruiz appeared to her and talked of her roses and how she had planted lovely flowers. So Brigita picked the yellow roses and handed her a bouquet. As they were talking, Maria asked if Brigita wanted to meet her daughter-in-law. Of course she did, and Maria called to Antonia to join them. The three ladies conversed at length about the garden and the house before Maria and Antonia departed, leaving Brigita breathless with her experience.

When Fernando came home he expected to find Brigita finishing with preparations for a dinner party. He couldn't understand why she wasn't dressed, and when she tried to explain her encounter in the garden, he refused to believe her. He went off to get her a glass of wine to calm her nerves. While he was out of the room a good friend, Mr. Alverez, came to the door. Brigita told Mr. Alverez about her experience and he, too, refused to believe her.

"My dear lady," he said, "It is just a figment of your imagination. Try to put it away from you."

She said, "He has promised me the house if I would stop talking about the spirits. I want the house. I don't want to give it up. But, this was so real."

They talked for a while, and finally he left her. As he reached the gate he stepped on a bouquet of freshly picked yellow roses. Slowly he returned to the house. "You must have dropped these," he suggested softly, presenting the bouquet to Brigita.

Her face was pale as she held the flowers tenderly, whispering only, "Maria's roses. Maria's yellow roses."

The story remains a legacy left by Eleanor Philips Barnes, who loved the history of the town and helped create traditions including the annual crowning of the Royal Family. The Royal Family represents the ruling family in Spain in 1672, the year the construction began on the Castillo de San Marcos. The family must have Spanish or Minorcan heritage and pledge to promote St. Augustine in numerous locations during their year of reign.

The facts behind the legends of the historic house on St. George Street remain clear. Luis Benedit y Horruytiner was governor of Spanish Florida from 1633 to 1638. His brother, Mosen Gilbert Benedit y Horruytiner, was a rancher in Florida with lands along the St. Johns River. His son, Pedro Alcantara Benedit Horruytiner, the nephew of Luis, was governor of Florida from 1646 to 1648.

The ownership of the Horruytiner House has been thoroughly documented. Masonry portions of the house date from the first Spanish Period, connecting the two governors to the property and the house. Don Pedro Alcantara Benedit Horruytiner y Pueyo did indeed live in the house in 1763, selling it the following year to a Spaniard, Juan Elixio de la Puente, who had been appointed by the king to dispose of Spanish property at the outset of the British Period. The house changed hands many times until it was purchased by Fernando de La Maza Arrendondo in 1801. Arrendondo was an aide to Governor Vicente Manuel de Zespedes and probably did keep his promise to Brigita. The house was not sold until 1839, when Virginia Watson purchased the structure by auction.[3]

THE SPANISH GENTLEMAN

The stories of the house with the name few people can pronounce (remember "Ooo-root-tin-air"?) continue to crop up. As I was working on this book, a friend from years ago, Danielle, called and said she had a story about her mother. I invited her over and listened as she told me about her mother, Jenny, living in a big masonry structure. Her mother was a no-nonsense woman who didn't believe in ghosts. But Danielle remembers Jenny being concerned about several incidents. The first was hearing her daughter come home from a date and ascend the staircase. But no one was there. Later a friend was in the kitchen washing dishes when she heard someone descending the stairs, then pausing at the landing. She checked, and no one was visible. The incidents reached a peak when Jenny felt the presence of someone walk up behind her in the front parlor. She turned around and saw no one. This was more frightening to her than someone being in the room.

She decided she'd had enough: "My mother stood in the middle of the room and turned to the north corner, telling the ghost to go away. She did that at each corner until she felt comfortable she had rid her house of the pesky intruder."

Well, it did not take. Danielle's mother never said much more about the ghost, but she suddenly decided they were going to leave. She never went back to the house.

Danielle never lived in the house herself, so she was relying on memories of verbal descriptions. Her family does not talk about it much, but the stories about the house remain in a variety of versions. Legends are made by repetition. If people did not continue to repeat sightings of Bigfoot or the Loch Ness Monster, the fables would fade from our memories. The same applies to the legends in the Horruytiner House.

After Danielle finished her stories, I shared this story with her about a sighting in the Horruytiner House parlor told to me by Maggie Patterson, a longtime owner of the house. The incident started when Maggie's grandson became agitated and ran from the parlor, visibly frightened. As Maggie went to investigate, she clearly saw a figure dressed in clothing she described as "cavalier boots and a plumbed hat." The clothing she saw was consistent with styles of the 1600s to 1700s, the time period of Don Pedro Benedit de Horruytiner, the Spanish governor of Florida from 1646 to 1648 and again from 1651 to 1654.

Although Maggie could describe the clothing she saw, dating it and identifying the gentleman came later when Maggie was sorting through a box left behind by a previous owner. In it she found a photograph of an actor portraying Don Pedro Horruytiner. He was dressed in the clothing she envisioned in the image of the Spanish gentleman. She is certain she and her grandson were visited by the long-dead governor.

ANDREW RANSON'S NEAR-DEATH EXPERIENCE

The story of Andrew Ranson is a pirate story, but he was also an experienced cannoneer and engineer. According to a National Park Service Interpretive Series, "The old time gunner was not only an artist, vastly superior to the average soldier, but, when circumstances permitted, he performed his wizardry with all due ceremony."

The ceremony of the gunner is repeated at the Castillo de San Marcos on a regular basis and relates to Ranson. The explanation follows:

> Gunners had no trouble finding work, as is singularly illustrated by the case of Andrew Ransom [sic], a stray Englishman captured near St. Augustine in the late 1600s. He was condemned to death. The execution device failed, however, and the padres in attendance took it as an act of God and led Ransom to sanctuary at the friary. Meanwhile, the Spanish governor learned this man was an artillerist and a maker of "artificial fires." The governor offered to "protect" him if he

would live at the Castillo and put his talents to use. Ransom did.[4]

Today the story is told as a pirate story. From as early as 1586 when Sir Francis Drake raided St. Augustine, the little garrison town had been besieged by pirates. Rarely were the attackers caught, but once in 1684 a group of pirates finally was captured. The celebrated event occurred on the other side of the inlet in a place we now call Vilano Beach. Town officials felt they should make an example of the villainous pirates so other ocean outlaws would be less likely to disturb the peaceful town.

The officials chose to publicly execute the pirates in the town plaza. The method chosen was garroting. This was a painful and lengthy means of execution, far worse than a simple hanging. A rope was tied around the criminal's neck and slowly tightened so, little by little, the effects of strangulation took effect. As the executioner turned the rope, the prisoner felt the loss of breath, then dizziness, then finally death. The spectators could watch as the face became blue and the eyes bulged from the sockets. It was exactly the procedure the officials desired for these scourges of the sea.

The leader of the group was Andrew Ranson. He was forced to witness the execution of the other pirates before his sentence was administered. He stood before the executioner calmly as the rope was placed around his neck. He remained composed as it was tightened once, twice, three times, and by the fourth time he lost consciousness. One more turn and it was almost over. Then the executioner twisted the rope one last turn. But the rope didn't tighten. Instead it snapped in two. To the amazement of the spectators, Andrew Ranson fell to the ground and began breathing. The Catholic priest in attendance walked to the body and slowly rolled it over. From Ranson's neck hung a small metal cross.

"This man is a Christian," exclaimed the priest. "Spare him from death!" And Andrew Ranson was spared. Not only was he given life, but he was given a purpose for living. It was determined that he had extraordinary engineering and artillery skills, and his talents were put to work on the construction of the Castillo de San Marcos. He became a productive member of society, met and married a woman of the town, and fathered several children. To this day, ancestors of this former pirate reside in this town. Andrew Ranson was given a second chance. And, as far as we know, none of his children became pirates.

According to maritime historian Cindy Vallar, Ranson was an Englishman born around 1650. He arrived in the West Indies when he was in his twenties and soon ended up in a Cuban prison. In 1684 he signed on with Captain Thomas Jingle to raid Spanish Florida.[5]

Six ships set sail with the objective of raiding St. Augustine in 1683. As frequently happens in sea stories, a storm was brewing as the ships neared the northeast coast of Spanish Florida. When the treacherous winds finally abated, only one ship remained. That ship sent smaller vessels ashore around the present-day Palm Valley/Ponte Vedra area to obtain supplies. Cattle ranchers alerted Spanish soldiers to the presence of the buccaneers' ship, and Ranson and several of his shipmates were captured and taken to St. Augustine. The story of the failed execution is true, as are the facts following the survival of the doomed pirate. He became significant in the building of the Castillo de San Marcos and apparently was an excellent gunner. Records of him disappear after the siege of 1702 by Governor James Moore of the Carolinas. Although we cannot be certain, it is a nice piece of the story to imagine the Englishman Ranson on the gun deck firing at the British in defense of Spanish St. Augustine. It is a story with twists and turns that earns it a prominent place in our cultural history.

2

MINORCAN
CULTURE

THE SANCHEZ GHOSTS' LAMENT FOR ANNIE LAURIE

St. Augustine's Minorcan stories and legends include a poem by Ann Browning Masters. "The Sanchez Ghosts' Lament for Annie Laurie" reflects the fierce determination to maintain a culture isolated from others. Masters notes that Annie Laurie suffered indignities from her in-laws. She wrote, "Since they're all in heaven now revisionist history can speculate that the Sanchez ghosts of Holy Branch sing a lament for her sorrows."

A quote from a Minorcan identified only as "Anonymous relative" follows: "Hard-shell Baptist Annie Laurie Ivey went up in those cradle-Catholics at Holy Branch and married Charley Sanchez. She was outnumbered and outflanked from day one."

Ann Browning Masters expressed her feeling poetically.

Forgive our ways, dear Annie Laurie.
We truly thought that we were right.
This was our home a hundred years.
We had our pride. We had our might.

Forgive our ways, dear Annie Laurie,
For they were harsh and clannish ways.
Ought should live as then you did
In your new and married days.

Forgive our ways, dear Annie Laurie,
So fair and brave, unlike our own.
We did not know to give much care
To one so far away from home.

Forgive our ways, dear Annie Laurie,
Blue-eyed bride whom we gave pain.
If only we could bid you love,
Or time could bring you here again.

If only we could bid you love,
Or time could bring you here again.

According to Michelle Reyna, a Minorcan native and active costumed role-player and historic interpreter of Minorcan culture, the Minorcans were very private people who kept their stories close to home. She agreed that ghost stories were never told openly, but were whispered throughout the generations.

PAFFE HOUSE: THE NUN, THE NURSE, AND THE SOLDIER

This spooky but charming story takes place on property once owned by a Minorcan family. The Spanish arrived on Florida's shores in 1565 and stayed until 1821 with the exception of the twenty-year occupation of the British from 1763 to 1784. Siblings Don Parry and Eileen Colvin explained the connection of the Paffe name to the Minorcan heritage. They said Paffe is from German ancestry. Parry related that "two brothers came over from Hamburg and settled in Trenton, New Jersey." He continued, "One of them ended up moving to St Augustine and marrying into the Minorcan invasion! My parents 'upline' includes a Triay-Carrera (Mom's side) and a Triay-Hernandez on Dad's side."

The family names include several Clements and Josephs, so sorting through the similar names was difficult. The story, however, rings true. The following is one version.

Maggie Hunter was a dedicated nurse with a soft spot in her heart for the elderly matriarch of the Paffe family. It was not unusual for her to visit at different hours, and on this particular dark and stormy night in 1927 Maggie felt she should check on her charge. She let herself into the house, ascending the stairs to the apartments above the shops. As she walked to the end of the hall where the grandmother's bedroom was, she was startled to see the image of a religious figure wearing the habit of the Sisters of St. Joseph. The nun was fingering rosary beads as she knelt by the elderly lady. As suddenly as the image appeared, it vanished from sight.

The presence of the nun was so unexpected, Maggie fled down the hall to the room of the grandson, Clement, who was a ham radio operator. Breathlessly, she told him what she had seen.

After calming Maggie, Clement explained that the "nun" was there to tend to his grandmother's needs. She was welcome in the house. He told Maggie not to worry, and she accepted his words of assurance.

When Maggie returned to the room, she found the grandmother resting comfortably in her bed. There was no sign of the nun's presence. As the days progressed Maggie frequently observed the nun near the door when she arrived; then the image disappeared. She noticed that the nun most often appeared when the elderly woman was in distress. Soon Maggie became accustomed to the existence of the spiritual entity and found solace in her presence.

Then one day Maggie arrived and, upon reaching the grand-mother's room, was shocked to see a Spanish soldier standing at the door as if on guard.

Maggie hastened to the grandson's room, expecting to hear some sort of an explanation for the phenomenon. Instead Clement raced down the hall, yelling. He threw open the door to his grandmother's room and ran inside, only to find her lying in her bed—dead.

When he recovered enough to talk to Maggie he explained that legends in their family told of the nun coming to provide comfort to the sick and dying. "But," Clement said, "When you see the soldier, he has come to take the person to the other side."

The sentimental story of the nun, the nurse, and the Spanish soldier is often told near the building at 53 St. George Street. The structure, which was originally constructed as the Pellicer–Peso de Burgo House honoring two Minorcan families, now houses the Bull and Crown Publick House. Constructed by the Historic St. Augustine Preservation Board in 1974, the building used a 49 St. George Street address and went through numerous phases, including a period when it served as the entrance to the Spanish Quarter Museum.

The story is about the Paffe family, who occupied a business and a home on that site. The large brick building occupied three lots, with 49 St. George Street housing a stationery store and print shop. Number 53 was assigned to the portion used as a toy store and card shop. Apartments above the shops used 51 St. George Street as their address.

When I first heard this story I called Joseph Paffe who, at the time, was teaching middle-school math. He impressed me as a very solid, down-to-earth person who I expected to disparage the legend. His response surprised me. "Oh, yes," he said.

"The grandson was my uncle Clement." He assured me that the story was known in the family to be true.

There are numerous versions of this story, some acted out with professional storytelling skills by Margaret Kaler. Some say the storm was the big hurricane of 1927. The story holds true in any rendering.

Don Parry added an interesting appendage to this tale. He said his grandfather was Fabian Joseph Paffe Sr., who in the 1920s was a world champion and world record holder in small-bore marksmanship. The world record targets are engraved on the back of the headstone in San Lorenzo Cemetery. The Paffe name will definitely be carried on in St. Augustine's history.

KENNY BEESON'S EXORCISM RITE

It wasn't the mysterious smells that put Kenny Beeson, a Minorcan, over the edge. Nor was it the sounds of booted feet stamping across the floor, or the ship's bell that rang when no one entered the shop door.

No, it was when his friend died in the 1960s and he couldn't banish the spirits from his shop. That's when he knew he had to take the next extraordinary step. He had to ask a Catholic priest to exorcise the evil spirits invading his life.

It all started when Kenny was a young man working as a tailor at Kixie's Men's Store at 138 St. George Street. Only Kenny could smell the perfumed odors in the back workroom. Then came the sounds: stamping feet, a ringing bell over the front door, even moaning and the sound of clanging chains.

It was becoming difficult to work alone at night, so when Kenny's friend Preston kept him company one night, he was relaxed. That is, until the bathroom door slowly swung open and an overwhelmingly sweet odor drifted through the air.

"We're getting out of here," Kenny yelled. The two men sprang to their feet, but before Preston went through the door Kenny noticed the image of a face on the back of his shirt. It was too late to stop him as Preston was hightailing it out to the parking lot. But Kenny paused long enough to pull out a tape recorder and leave it running on the workbench.

The next day he listened in awe as he heard the documented clamor. Before he could contact Preston, his friend died of a heart attack. It took all of his strength to attend the funeral, and as he entered the chapel he was overcome by the stench of funeral flowers, the same smell that had invaded his work space. Then he saw the man whose image had been emblazoned on the back of Preston's shirt. It was Preston's brother. Had this been a premonition of the death? The brother followed his sibling in death soon thereafter.

Kenny was so shaken by all of the strange events that he went to Monsignor Harold Jordan to ask for help. Although Monsignor Jordan had never attempted an exorcism rite, he realized how deeply frightened Kenny was. He blessed the rooms and ordered the demonic spirits to leave.

The service apparently worked as all was quiet after that. Kenny said he never heard anything else, although occasionally he did smell flowers.

Kenny Beeson became an admired leader in the community, serving two terms as city mayor. He taught classes about Minorcan history and had his master's thesis printed as the book *Fromajadas and Indigo*. He chose to keep his story quiet, telling it only to his closest friends. It was not until 1992 when he went public with the story, telling it to me for publication in the *St. Augustine Record*'s arts-and-entertainment section,

"The Compass." From there it has become one of the staples of the ghost-tour litany of tales.

Exorcism is not that unusual in the Catholic religion. As it relates to the local story, Kenny Beeson was a friend of Monsignor Jordan who, though not trained in the exorcism procedure, agreed to cleanse the property of evil spirits. It is generally believed that exorcism had not been used previously in the St. Augustine Catholic Church parish. This was a remarkable request for a heritage native and member of the Catholic congregation.

The most famous story of exorcism is the movie *The Exorcist*, released in 1973. The book and movie were based on a real event. The reality of the production was made clear to me when a local neurosurgeon told me he had known the priest who performed the exorcism. The priest's identity is well known today. He is Father Gabriele Amorth, who performed hundreds of exorcisms before he died in 2016. Exorcism, or the cleansing of spirits, is well known today.

Kenny Beeson had every right to be afraid of his "spirits." It was fortunate for him that Monsignor Jordan was able to rid the St. George Street shop of the intruders. Or did he?

Shortly after the story was printed, a couple living in an apartment down the street from Kixie's Men's Store came to me with their tale of strange events in their residence. Is it possible that the spirit occupying Kixie's moved down the street? Read on.

CHAMP AND THE RED BLOUSE

The story of Champ and the red blouse necessitates repeating due to its connection with the Beeson story. Shortly after

Beeson's story was printed in the St. Augustine Record, I was approached by a couple who owned a store called Champ's Deli on Aviles Street. The deli was named for a big, white, fluffy Eskimo Spitz whose image was used as the logo for the restaurant. The owners, Bob and Diane Sims, came to me very distressed. Champ, old and blind, was walking on the second-floor patio of their second-story apartment, a few yards away from Kixie's Men's Store, when he suddenly fell. The owners said he knew the boundaries and would not have fallen unless something unusual happened. They didn't know how or why the dog fell but hadn't questioned it until a newly acquired Pomeranian began acting strangely. Bob said it looked like a large animal was grabbing the miniature in its mouth and shaking him. The assumption was that Champ had returned from the dead and was jealously guarding his territory.

The Simses knew the Kenny Beeson story but did not believe it had any connection to the death of Champ until more strange incidents occurred. The first occurrence was the red blouse. The shirt was a gift to Diane that she never wore. She said she didn't like red. The clothing item was lying on the bed when she returned home from work one day. She knew she had never taken the item from the closet, and Bob vehemently denied any knowledge of it. That incident was followed by items being moved in the house that neither Bob nor Diane claimed to have moved.

As all the items were being moved, the little dog continued to have convulsions. The couple was distraught. A psychic visited the house with me and said very little until we were alone outside. She told me there were no ghosts in the apartment. She felt the little dog needed medical attention, and she was sure there was some explanation for the red blouse and the other items being moved that was not paranormal activity.

I discussed some of this with Bob and Diane, who took the little dog to a vet. They found the dog suffered from seizures resulting in the unusual behavior and could recover with medical treatment. As the mystery unfolded, a teenager was arrested for entering apartments in the area and simply moving items around as he searched for valuables to steal.

This story turned out to be a tale with no ghosts. No one can say why the elderly, blind Champ fell off the building. What is known is that the little dog was not being shaken by the jaws of a jealous ghost dog, and he did recover. The teenager roaming the neighborhood apartments was arrested and admitted to his petty crimes.

Did Kenny Beeson's ghost haunt the Simses' apartment? Probably not. Kenny's ghost was exorcised off the street, and everything has remained calm as far as I know. But then, what do I know?

BENET STORE ACTIVITY

The Benet Store, 62 St. George Street, draws customers for its eclectic line of gift items, but also due to its name recognition. The Benet name is known today for literary talents Steven Vincent Benét and his siblings Laura and William. The name also is associated with the Minorcan settlers in St. Augustine. The family did not immigrate with the Turnbull indentured servants but came from San Filipe, Minorca, the port town that had been home to many of the indentured servants. In 1796 Esteban Benét disembarked from a sailing vessel in St. Augustine to be welcomed by Minorcans from his hometown. His uncle was an important officer in the Spanish Navy, stationed in Havana. Esteban stayed in St.

Augustine and married Catalina Hernandez. They produced a child, Pedro Benét, who became a leader in the Minorcan community and was given the unofficial title of "king of the Minorcans."

In recent years Marla Pennington, owner of the Benet Store, reported numerous incidents in the shop. The shop was originally planned to represent a territorial time period, 1821–45, the years before Florida gained statehood.

It was in the 1980s when Marla had an encounter with a territorial-period ghost. She was setting up the counter when she noticed a woman shopping. The woman wore a long dress and held a basket in her hand. She appeared as a solid figure to Marla. As Marla watched, a little boy dressed in 1840s clothing appeared in the doorway, running to the woman, most likely his mother. Both moved toward the back door and disappeared as they entered the courtyard, vanishing into the air. Following that appearance, workers in the store often reported the sounds of laughter in the courtyard and children singing old-fashioned nursery rhymes. Perhaps the time warp was repeated by the children of the era.

The stories in the Benet Store continue beyond the territorial-ghost sightings. Marla bought the Dreamweaver store adjacent to the Benet Store. It was in this building that the poodles appeared. Two little white curly-haired dogs were often seen on the steps of the building. Marla knew they were not real. They would disappear in an eyeblink. But she did not mind their presence. What was unusual was the presence of a lady shopping in the store who told Marla her grandparents had lived there years before. As the woman reminisced, she commented that her grandparents had two white poodles. Both women were startled by the events that could not be considered a simple coincidence. The little white dogs wanted to stay in the home they loved.

Marla also encountered a ghost with a bad attitude. When a certain man often appeared on the steps, Marla said she always "felt a chill." The man, whose identity was not revealed to Marla, would materialize on the stairs and block her way in a threatening manner. Finally, frustrated and angry, she told him to go away. To her relief and surprise, he left, never to appear to her again.

The Benét name will always be remembered beyond the streets of St. Augustine. Who knows why the poodles persist in being recognized?

CAROL LOPEZ: PEACE OUT

Carol Lopez Bradshaw is a heritage native dedicated to Minorcan history and culture. She is one of the founders of the Menorcan Society, a group which chooses to spell the name with "e" instead of "i" to reflect the Spanish spelling.

Carol lives on a street in downtown St. Augustine with homes occupied by families of Minorcan heritage. The Minorcan culture is based on the Catholic religion. According to Carol and Minorcan Michelle Reyna, "We don't believe in ghosts." That said, both participated in the ghost tours and ultimately had their own stories. Carol's story is extremely unusual and unexplainable.

With Carol's firm Catholic upbringing and an understanding of a cultural norm rejecting ghosts, her experience was not only frightening, it was beyond comprehension. As Carol told the story to me when I visited the house, I learned that something unworldly was written on the bathroom mirror. When mist was in the room and Carol left the shower, the words "Peace Out" were written on the window. This happened more than once. Paranormal experts came to the house and no one could determine any specific reason for the message. Carol, a strong woman, told the spirit to go away. No ghost busters helped her rid the house of the unwanted spirits. It was up to Carol to drive them out, and she commanded them to leave.

Carol's family, friends, and neighbors know that the event happened. Everyone believes it. Now, all that Carol wants is to be "at peace" in her own home. We all hope she will be.

ALONZO "LON" MANUCY: A GRANDMOTHER'S SENSE

Another Minorcan story is that of Lon Manucy's experience. His story is where legends begin, and generations of Manucy family members will repeat it.

Lon Manucy was on a hunting expedition in 1973 when he was nineteen years old. An accident occurred, and the injured young man was rushed to the hospital with serious injuries that resulted in the amputation of his arm.

Information about the tragedy was withheld from Lon's grandmother until Lon was recovering from surgery. But she knew something serious had happened because of the chiming clock. The timepiece, a pretty ornament but nonfunctional, had alerted Lon's grandmother in 1965 to the death of her husband, Lon's grandfather. According to Lon, the clock chimed so loudly his grandmother had to turn it on its side to stop it from ringing. When Lon was injured, the clock started chiming and the grandmother knew a tragedy had occurred.

When she learned of her grandson's accident, she calmly replied she knew something bad had happened; she just did not know what it was. Fortunately, Lon recovered from his injuries and is living a happy and productive life.

With that difficult experience behind them, Lon and his wife, Debbie, were also victims of a demonic encounter. The young couple had a sincere faith in God and had finished watching a spiritual TV show, *The 700 Club*, when demonic forces entered their home. They had read biblical scriptures before retiring to bed. It was Lon who first felt the presence of the evil spirits. He was awakened during the night with the sensation of hands squeezing his neck. He said, "In the name of Jesus." The pressure was released. Lon awakened Debbie, and they both talked about the terrifying experience before falling asleep again. Then it was Debbie who was attacked by demonic forces. The choking sensation began in a manner similar to Lon's experience. She felt hands around her neck clutching her so tightly she could not scream. When the sensation abated, she roused Lon and the two of them walked through the house reciting biblical scriptures. When they reached the living room a lamp began to sway wildly. Debbie said it was "hitting the walls and banging back and forth." Finally it stopped and everything was quiet. The young couple left the house with their faith strengthened by the terrifying experiences.

Most of the stories about paranormal activity are benign and often tell us something about the people involved. Demonic tales are exactly that—evil at work. The people telling these stories were clearly frightened and quickly removed themselves from a difficult situation.

3

INTO
TERRITORIAL
DAYS

FATHER VARELA AND BISHOP VEROT:
BURIED TOGETHER

There is a little chapel mausoleum in the back of Tolomato Cemetery on Cordova Street. Visitors can tour the building when the grounds are open, and guides are available to tell the story about the Catholic priest and a bishop whose earthly remains have occupied the room. It is an interesting and informative experience when the doors are open and sunlight brightens the interior.

But at night, when it is dark, strange things happen. Lights appear inside the chapel although no electricity is available. "Who is in there?" customers ask on the ghost tours. "No one," is the reply.

The occasional appearance of eerie lights is not what excites the crowd. That is just show stuff. It is the story of the "exploding bishop" and the poor priest whose bones were removed and put in a pillow case. The tale can be told with dramatically gruesome details, and the people who paid for entertainment love it. How much is true? Far more than one might expect.

In order to understand the events that took place over the years from the time of the deaths of Father Varela and Bishop Verot until recent years, one must understand who the two men were and what happened after their deaths.

Félix Francisco José Varela y Morales was born in Havana, Cuba, in 1788. Though Cuban by birth, he was raised in St. Augustine by his grandfather Lieutenant Bartolomé Morales, the commander of military forces in Spanish Florida. Morales was stationed in the garrison town that became home to the boy who grew up to be an ordained Catholic priest, an educator, and a fighter for Cuban liberty from Spain.

Varela returned to Cuba for formal education while still a teenager and, by age twenty-two, was ordained as a priest. Within a year of ordination, he became a member of the faculty of San Ambrosio Seminary, teaching philosophy, physics, and chemistry.

By 1821 Varela was firmly embroiled in the fight for Cuba's independence from Spanish rule. His actions ultimately led to a death sentence; however, he managed to escape and fled to the United States, where he settled in New York.

His many accomplishments while in the Empire State included the position of vicar general of the Diocese of New York, which covered all of New York State and the northern half of New Jersey.

In 1848 Varela returned to St. Augustine, ill with asthma. He was comfortable in his boyhood home because of his familiarity with the town. He also could connect with history in the Ancient City because St. Augustine also had been "liberated" from Spain when it became a territory of the United States in 1821, the same time period when Varela was liberating Cuba. Exhausted from years of work, the religious man died in 1853. He was buried in the Tolomato Cemetery. An impressive chapel-style mausoleum was built to honor the beloved priest, who later was chosen to be elevated to sainthood by the Catholic Church.

Father Varela was honored with a commemorative U.S. postal stamp issued in St. Augustine in 1997. A monument in the Plaza de la Constitución commemorates the popular priest.

Jean-Pierre Augustine Marcellin Verot was born in Le Puy-en-Velay, France, in 1805. He became the first bishop of the Diocese of St. Augustine in 1870, serving in that capacity until his death in 1876. His death came twenty-three years after Father Varela's demise.[1]

Bishop Verot died in June 1876 during a hot summer day. It was necessary to postpone a formal funeral until Catholic dignitaries from distant locations could arrive. The well-respected bishop of St. Augustine was laid to rest in a metal coffin. A glass plate permitted viewers to see his face as they paid their last respects. As the congregation and residents waited, the hot weather took its toll on the dead body. According to many accounts, the body "exploded," and glass flew through the church.

Although versions of the event are written about and repeated with grotesque details, the reality is the glass on top of the metal casket did indeed shatter, but without the gory depictions. It became necessary to quickly move the casket from the church to the Tolomato Cemetery. The most expedient action was taken to remove the lid from the tomb of Father Varela, extract his remains, and place them in a corner of the chapel so the good Bishop could be placed in the existing crypt.

That remained the situation for years with locked doors protecting the two prelates. Then, in 1911, a delegation from Spain came to St. Augustine, demanding the remains of the Cuban hero. The remains were moved to Cuba. The question arose, however, about the certainty of whose bones the Cubans had and who lay entombed inside the chapel mausoleum constructed for Father Varela. In 1970 the crypt was once again opened with church representatives, including priest and historian Father Michael Gannon, inspecting the remains. Father Gannon recognized the cross in the casket as the one Verot would have worn at the time of the funeral.[2]

Once the identities were established, more work was required to effectively resolve the issues. In 1987 a new tomb was built for Bishop Verot in the center of the cemetery. The bishop's casket was removed from the crypt and placed in a granite vault visible from Cordova Street. A bronze bust of the bishop created by sculptor Ted Karam overlooks the casket.

The history of the mausoleum, referred to as the Varela Chapel, is fascinating in and of itself. After Varela's death he was buried beside his aunt, Rita Morales, as construction proceeded on the chapel. The Cuban delegation ordered mahogany for an altar and Cuban marble for a tablet and a cover for the crypt. A translation of the plaque states, "This chapel was built by the Cubans in 1853 to preserve the remains of Fr. Varela."

Indigenous coquina stone was used for construction, and the chapel was completed in 1855 when Varela's remains were moved to what was then believed to be his final resting place.

The chapel stood empty and locked until recent years. The Varela Chapel now has been beautifully restored by the Tolomato Cemetery Preservation Association and can be visited when the grounds are open. A replica of the original altar contains a corbel of the former altar as it was carved in Havana in the 1850s.[3]

Father Varela and Bishop Verot were revered by many people beyond the limits of St. Augustine. Father Varela is being considered for canonization as a Catholic saint. The process requires several steps before canonizations can be bestowed on him. He is already considered a servant of God, recognizing his life as a devoted Catholic.

Here in our little town we keep their memories alive with their stories. It would be respectful if those stories were told with more truth than drama.

The Tolomato Cemetery is open the third Saturday of every month, with guides available to explain the stories.

THE OPOPANAX TREE

Regardless of the amount of research conducted, I found no source or reason for the story of the opopanax tree (sometimes spelled "apopinax" in stories). The tale involves a Spanish lady of means who presumably died. She was carried in a chair to the Tolomato Cemetery, the assumption being that this is a Spanish custom. I have found no evidence of that being traditional.

According to the story, the woman's husband and lover were with her, and, when the funeral procession reached the cemetery, a thorn from the opopanax tree scraped her throat. The lover, a respected judge in the community, saw blood seeping from the cut. He yelled to stop the funeral ceremony, and the deceased was found to be quite alive.

The story continues with the woman living for several years before dying once again. As they carried her a second time to the burial plot, the husband pushed away the lover, ordering the chair carriers to move away from the tree. He did not want a repeat of past performances. This time the burial was completed, whether she was dead or not.

The story can be an entertaining dramatic presentation, but I can find nothing to substantiate it. Most people with Spanish heritage have repudiated the story.

THE WORTH HOUSE: O. C. WHITE'S RESTAURANT

The greatest crab cakes in the oldest city can be found at O. C. White's restaurant, cooked from a recipe created by the owner's wife, Cathy. What continues to be remarkable about the eating establishment is not just the food, but the ambiance and history. Today it is listed as O. C. White's Seafood and Spirits, probably because it has more "spirits" roaming the historic building than spirits found at the bar.

Owner David White relates a story about a fire in the building shortly after he opened it as a restaurant. He hung a picture of the building as it appeared when it was owned by Margaret Worth, the wife of General William Jenkins Worth. The general, an admired military man, served during the Seminole Indian Wars and lived in Florida for several years. He died in 1849 of cholera and was buried in Texas before his remains were reinterred below a fifty-one-foot granite monument in Manhattan, New York. Fort Worth, Texas, and numerous cities and landmarks honor the soldier.

After the general's death, Margaret moved to St. Augustine and purchased a building on the west side of current Marine Street, approximately on the location of the parking lot for O. C. White's restaurant. The structure dated to 1791 and had been renovated for use as a hotel. Margaret restored it as a private dwelling, and her daughter, Mary, and Mary's husband, Col. John T. Sprague, came to live in the home until Margaret died in 1869. The building remained in the Worth family until

1904. In 1948 the home was purchased by George L. Potter, of Potter's Wax Museum fame. He elected to move the structure stone-by-stone across the street to its present location. For a short time it was a Wendy's chain restaurant, but that was unsuccessful. Perhaps people stopping for fast food do not wish to be bothered by ghosts. The hauntings are attributed to Margaret Worth or to Mary Sprague and her husband.

White said by the time he was alerted to the fire on the third floor of the building everything in his office was burned. His cameras were ruined, and the liquor stored in the area had exploded. The only item remaining untouched was the photo of the building, which remained intact in a wooden frame. There is a certain amount of emotion when White tells his story. There has never been a clear understanding of the cause of the fire, but the stories of hauntings remain.

One employee reported looking through a recipe box when she was called away from the work space. Upon returning she found the cards tossed along the countertop. She replaced the cards, only to leave again before selecting the desired recipes. When she returned a second time, the cards had been thrown around haphazardly. There was no explanation for the flying recipe cards. It was one more strange occurrence in the restaurant.

Another employee, Van, told the story of a broken necklace. The necklace was made from a string of beads and given to her by her daughter. It was small and had to be rolled down her head to wear it comfortably. Van was concerned that it was so small she might have to cut it to take it off. After a few hours at work Van touched her neck and realized the beads were missing. Her immediate concern was to locate the baubles so no customers would trip on them. She searched without finding any sign of the little jewels. Toward the end of the day a coworker approached, swinging the necklace on her finger-tips. Shocked, Van asked where the colleague had found it. The answer was mystifying. The necklace was hanging from a doorknob on the third floor. Van had never approached the area, nor had anyone working with her. It was a mystery with no answer unless Margaret or Mary liked the little beads.

Although there have been sightings of women in white walking the halls and voices heard when no one is around, it is the strange movement of pots and pans and cutlery that keeps everyone wondering. Knives and forks placed in con-tainers in preparation for washing have been lifted straight up and dropped into the sink. Pots and pans have tumbled down the stairs from a storage closet and landed in the kitchen. Nu-merous people have reported being hugged or pushed on the stairs going up to the second-floor eating area.

Although the food is wonderful in the popular dining estab-lishment, it seems the ghosts provide the most entertainment.

OSCEOLA

Osceola, the infamous Seminole Indian warrior, did indeed lose his head to a surgeon's knife. The bizarre part of the story is that his head was cut off in Fort Moultrie, South Carolina, in 1838. It was then embalmed and transferred back to St. Augustine. Years later, it was given to a museum in New York and was ultimately lost in a fire.

Why then do people see his image imprinted on the co-quina stone of the Castillo de San Marcos? Why do visitors claim to see the head floating over the fort like a moon rising from the ocean? Legends abound concerning the death of the often celebrated Seminole warrior, who was imprisoned in the

Look carefully for the image of Native American Osceola that visitors see on the Castillo de San Marco Wall. Photo courtesy of Tour St. Augustine.

Castillo de San Marcos in 1837. Reality and legends blend with those stories of Osceola's head.

Although Osceola was held captive in the fort, he did not die there. He was moved to Fort Moultrie, South Carolina, in a weakened condition resulting from malaria. His doctor, Frederick Weedon, accompanied him. It is known that Weedon was with him at the time of death. It is also known that Osceola's head was severed from his body after his demise.

Apparently, Weedon returned to St. Augustine with the cranium. Stories are told that the doctor hung the head on his children's bedposts to punish them when they misbehaved.

There is a house on the corner of Bridge and Weedon streets where Dr. Frederick Weedon is said to have lived with his family. In the 1990s a little boy was visiting his grandfather in that house. The youngster was awakened in the bedroom, startled by the figure of a tall Indian peering over his bed. Although surprised, he was not frightened and reported the vision to his grandfather in the morning. The grandfather was unwilling to admit that he knew the legend of Osceola's head and that Dr. Weedon would discipline his children by placing the disembodied head in the room at night. Perhaps he feared the grandson would not return for a visit.

The only problem with that story is that the house was not built until 1925 and Weedon died in 1857. Perhaps, though, he did live on the street named for him and spirits exist. It is known that Weedon kept the embalmed head in his office or in a drugstore.

Facts continuing to authenticate the story include Weedon's presentation of the skull to his daughter and son-in-law as a wedding gift. Although seemingly preposterous, the fact is, the skull was a precious item historically and scientifically. Weedon's son-in-law, Daniel Whitehurst, studied medicine under Dr. Valentine Mott, a well-regarded surgeon in the country. Documentation shows that Whitehurst eventually presented Osceola's remains to Mott, who died in April 1865. Shortly after his death a fire consumed part of the Mott Museum, and no written account provides evidence of the location of the famous cranium.

4
STATEHOOD

ABBOTT MANSION

The worst possible scenario regarding ghosts involves physical contact and injury. The experience of Starr Gray while living in a third-floor apartment of Abbott Mansion on Joiner Street is frightening to anyone hearing the story.

Imagine falling down stairs and nearly being pushed out of a third-story window by a ghost. It happened to Starr. Starr and her husband, David, lasted only four months in the haunted house. They attribute what happened to Lucy Abbott, who lived from 1838 to 1929 and was the first female land developer in St. Augustine. There is no reason to believe Lucy was a malevolent person. She was a smart woman who bought land and constructed houses in what is now called Abbott Tract in the neighborhood on the north side of St. Augustine. She never married and enjoyed life as a successful businesswoman, with many friends in town. She lived to be ninety-one, and ironically the enterprising woman died the day before the stock market crashed in 1929.

Starr was convinced Lucy was in the house and didn't like her. The stories start with frequent knocking at the apartment door with no one outside when the door was opened. Footsteps were heard when no one was around. That is all typical haunting material, but what happened next goes beyond that. Starr began to feel a force pushing her down the stairs. She fell more than once and needed hospitalization for her injuries. During this time she heard a voice say, "Get out!" and she decided to do exactly that. She and David packed up to move and were almost out when Starr chose to lean out the apartment window to call to David. As she did a strong force pushed against her. She could barely stabilize herself, and, as the pressure mounted, she screamed for help. With great effort she moved herself back from the window. Visibly shaken, she walked out of the apartment for the last time.

The house that Lucy Abbott built was the first and the largest construction north of the City Gate. The address in an early city directory simply says, "The house north of the City Gate." Lucy lived there for a time but did not die in that house. The beautiful building went through many changes and in 2017 was purchased by Raul Rodriguez.

Vera Kramer ran a bed-and-breakfast in the building from 1980 until she finally sold all of her collections to Rodriguez. She did have some problems with ghosts, but mostly with clocks being turned on and off. She said the clocks with pendulums often stopped and started for no apparent reason. She had to push the pendulums to get them started. Only the battery-run clocks "never missed a tick."

Although not involving ghosts, an interesting addendum to Lucy Abbott's stories has to do with mules. As an astute businesswoman, Lucy was not about to be cheated out of anything.

As the Civil War erupted, Lucy's uncle James D. Starke, for whom the Florida town is named, sent two slaves and two mules to Lucy and his sister Margaret. During the Union occupation of Florida, Lucy's real-estate holdings and the two mules were confiscated. At the end of the war Lucy still did not have her land or her mules. She wrote to General Grant in 1868 requesting the return of her mules. She indicted her uncle was a "union man" who had been forced into Confederate service. At the end of the war Lucy still didn't have her land or her mules.

She wrote to General Grant:

> The right to the mules, such as it is, was released to me by my uncle who was their owner—I write this frank statement, on the truly distressing situation in which two women find themselves, to ask that this little property [be] given up to me for ou[r] benefit. I feel, General, that I am appealing to one of noble and generous impulses—to one who thought it not unmanly to weep at the downfall of an opponent, and cannot believe he will disregard the prayer of the unfortunate orphan.

Eventually, Lucy did regain her land, but never her mules.[1]

Lucy Abbott will always be remembered in St. Augustine, although not for the mules or the reputation as a ghost. She made a lasting impression in this town as a developer and a shrewd businesswoman. I suspect the mules were long gone by the time General Grant received her letter.

ABBIE BROOKS: MYSTERY WOMAN

Abbie Brooks, a mystery lady at the turn of the century in 1900, lurks in the halls of a house on Water Street. This is one story not told on the average ghost tours but is probably the most realistic story circulating around.

Abbie was a woman in her forties when she arrived in St. Augustine in the 1870s. She was alone and never divulged

This artist's rendition of Abbie Brooks hangs in the Casa Monica Resort & Spa on Cordova Street. Abbie Brooks's contributions to St. Augustine include the first guidebook for Florida. Painting by Marianne Lerbs. By permission of Richard Kessler.

personal information. In documents found after her death she described herself as "a waif floating about the shores of a fathomless sea." She had a passion for history and wrote what is considered to be the first guidebook of Florida. She titled it *Petals Plucked from Sunny Climes* and used the pseudonym Sylvia Sunshine.

I had heard that Abbie roamed around the house on Water Street where she resided when she died in 1914. Not everyone cares to talk about it. To my surprise, I met someone who lived in the house where Abbie died and had seen her. The meeting occurred one evening when I was entertaining a group of young girls in the gallery of the lightkeepers' house at St. Augustine Light House. I told ghost stories and, when I finished, a teenager came to me and told me she had a ghost in her house. I asked her if it was Abbie, and she said yes.

The connection was clear, and we both understood that Abbie was as real as a spirit could be. It was irrefutable. I knew Abbie, and so did the teenager.

Abbie Brooks was a mystery when she was alive because she never told anyone about her place of origin or her family. She simply existed. But exist she did. In addition to writing *Petals,* Abbie traveled to Spain and became the first American woman to research Florida's history in the archives of Seville and Madrid. Abbie is real.

Researchers Dick and Yvonne Punnett wanted to know more about the mysterious Abbie Brooks and spent years investigating her past. They discovered she had a child out of wedlock in the 1800s, when that was considered a disgrace. No one would blink twice about such a thing today. Abbie's child was named Ortie, and the Punnetts finally located her descendants. They have since visited Abbie's grave in Evergreen Cemetery. There is a portrait of Abbie in the Casa Monica hotel. The portrait was painted by Marianne Lerbs and depicts a strong-willed woman. Abbie was a mystery in life but is genuinely eager to be accepted and understood in her afterlife.

5

LIGHTHOUSE
ILLUMINATIONS

MARIA'S LAMENT

Maria Andreu was tending to winter vegetables in the garden of the lighthouse compound. There was a chill in the December air, but it was not too cold for her husband, Joseph, to be painting the tower that fateful day in 1859.

Maria heard a snap, then a bone-chilling bang when the body hit tin. As she turned she saw her husband roll from the roof of the oil shed, hitting the stone wall surrounding the compound. She and her three children ran to his body as the scaffolding dangled above them from the remaining rope. They gathered around their fallen loved one to no avail. Joseph died where he worked, leaving his wife to carry on the difficult duties of a lighthouse keeper.

Caring for the lighthouse was a family affair involving the constant transportation of whale oil or lard to the top of the tower, trimming the wicks, and maintaining the tower. In addition to those duties, detailed logs were kept and fruit and vegetables were grown in the nearby garden. It was a difficult, but not unpleasant, life for the Andreu family.

The city mourned the death of the lighthouse keeper. Joseph and Maria were both Minorcans who were known in the town. Now Maria, desolate and depressed, climbed the tower, carrying up a bucket of lard oil to the top. She felt alone and feared for her future. The night winds blew a light mist across her face as she gazed out to the ocean, praying a silent prayer for help. Then, throwing her arms to the elements, she wailed to the winds, crying out, "Joseph, what shall I do? What shall I do?"

The answer came as the rain began to fall. Joseph's voice, drifting with the wind. She heard, "Tend the light. Tend the light."

Visitors to the lighthouse pier often hear the voice of Maria calling in the wind, her anguished cries clear. Sometimes Joseph's reply can be heard above the gentle lapping of the ripples on the shore.

Maria's story is true, and she did elect to "tend the light" as her husband advised. She accepted her responsibility and was appointed by the United States government as the St. Augustine lighthouse keeper. She has been recognized as the first Hispanic-American woman to serve in the Coast Guard (or its predecessor services) and the first to command a federal shore installation.

In 1821, when Florida became a territory, the watchtower on Anastasia Island was recognized by the government as a potentially useful lighthouse. After repair work was completed, a lens was installed, and in 1824 the light was officially lit by Juan Andreu, a member of the Minorcan community and Joseph's cousin. It was understandable that a Minorcan would be appointed the first lighthouse keeper of the first lighthouse in Florida. They were seamen who knew the Florida shores and the mysteries of the sea.

Joseph Andreu became the fourth keeper in 1854. The year following his appointment, whale oil was replaced by lard, facilitating the task by reducing the weight of the fuel and producing a cleaner burn. Joseph lived and worked on the lighthouse compound with his wife, Maria de los Dolores Maestre, also of Minorcan heritage, and three of their numerous children.

When the Civil War reached Florida's borders, the light was extinguished in an effort to hinder Union naval operations off shore. Paul Arnau, the city's collector of customs, supervised the removal and disappearance of the Fresnel lens. With the lens gone, Maria was effectively out of work.

Today St. Augustine's famous striped lighthouse tower looms above Anastasia Island neighborhoods. That tower was completed in 1874, replacing the old coquina structure from the early 1700s.

It is believed Maria left St. Augustine around 1862 to live with a daughter in Georgia. However, her story and that of her husband are indelibly woven into the fabric of the oldest city's history. She had eight children, five of whom were adults at the time of the accident. Perhaps one of her descendents is reading this story and can come forward with a family version of the inspirational tale.

THE PITTEE ACCIDENT

The children knew they shouldn't play around construction equipment. The tram car sat on tracks sloping from the lighthouse tower to the roiling sea below. Riding the car was a tempting fun adventure and off-limits for the lively youngsters. But on July 10, 1873, on the construction site of the St. Augustine Lighthouse tower, fifteen-year-old Mary Pittee, allegedly clothed in a blue velvet dress, enticed her siblings and a friend to board the vehicle. Mary and Eliza, thirteen, encouraged younger siblings Edward and Carrie to climb on. The ten-year-old daughter of a black worker didn't hang back.

Then, something went horribly wrong. The vehicle took up speed and shot down the tracks, pitching forward when it hit the sand and pinning the children beneath it in the ocean waves. Workers scrambled to their aid and rescued Edward and Carrie. Mary, Eliza, and the little black girl, whose name we do not know, could not be saved.

Today Mary is seen, sometimes with such clarity that the blue velvet dress can be identified. Occasionally, she appears dripping wet. The two sisters often appear together around the light station. But, as far as we know, the little black girl has never been viewed.

During several months as a tour guide at the lighthouse I tried to see Mary and Eliza. Mary appears most often, frequently emerging in the second-floor window of the keeper's house. I would stand quietly waiting for her to materialize— she never did. Then, one summer day, I entertained a couple from Ohio who did see the girls, but not in my presence. After the tour, we left the grounds and drove off in different directions. What happened next prompted them to call me a week later from Ohio to tell me their story. They drove toward the pier, and, as they passed the playground, the car lights swept across a swing set. They saw the image of two girls playing on the swings. The couple stopped and pointed the lights toward them. The girls disappeared. They turned off the lights and could see the girls and hear the creak of the swings. After a few seconds the images disappeared, but the swings continued to move. Although mystified, the observers did not get out to investigate.

At another time, I was surprised to learn about a sighting by a young boy. It was daylight, and I was talking to some visitors on the lighthouse pier about the ghost girls. "I saw them over there," a youngster standing within earshot said, pointing to the keeper's house.

He said he saw them "on the steps," but I don't recall which steps he was referring to. The only steps inside the residence today lead to the basement. The steps to the second floor are outside the building. Regardless of the location, he clearly saw the Pittee sisters during the day. He did not see the little black girl.

Where is the little girl, and why can't we see her?

PETER RASMUSSEN: LONGEST LIGHTKEEPER

Sometimes unusual activity is experienced through the sense of smell, as happened with Kenny Beeson. (See "Kenny Beeson's Exorcism Rite" in chapter 2.) The St. Augustine Lighthouse and Museum has its unique story about people smelling cigar smoke. It is attributed to Peter Rasmussen, who transferred to the St. Augustine Lighthouse in 1901, becoming the longest keeper, with a record of twenty-three years of service.

Rasmussen worked from the office at the base of the tower. He was a heavy cigar smoker and regularly indulged his habit in the small room. The smell of cigar smoke has been documented by numerous employees and sometimes by visitors. One of the employees, Celeste, smelled the smoke before learning of Rasmussen's unhealthy practice. If the smoke smell was only associated with the office room, perhaps it could be explained as coming from a source nearby imitating a cigar-smoke smell. But it was not only in that room. It occurred in a gift shop near a former kitchen area and then later was smelled by a film crew on the grounds to document spiritual activity.

This author knew all of the stories but never expected to experience what I did. During a dedication ceremony at the lighthouse, rain poured from the sky. Visitors crowded on the back steps of the keeper's house, facing the tower. I was standing shoulder to shoulder with people trying to stay dry. Suddenly, I smelled the smoke. It was clearly cigar smoke. I asked the people beside me if they smelled it, and they said no. Why do some of us experience the phenomenon and others do not? I cannot answer that. I only know that I did smell the cigar smoke, and I believe that Peter Rasmussen wants to be remembered at the place he cherished for more than two decades of work. It is a strange way to be remembered, but we do talk about him because of it.

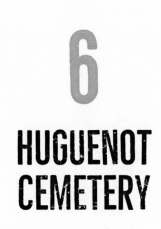

6

HUGUENOT
CEMETERY

THE HUGUENOT CEMETERY is the oldest Protestant cemetery in Florida. When Florida became a territory in 1821, the Spanish Catholics departed the former colony and Americans from northern states infiltrated the new land. Immediately a yellow fever epidemic destroyed lives, rapidly killing men and women of all ages. Since Protestants could not be buried in the Catholic Tolomato Cemetery, it was necessary to quickly find an appropriate burial spot. A plot of land just outside the City Gate was purchased as the Public Burial Ground and made available to all Protestants. As the years progressed, the cemetery was purchased by the St. Augustine Presbyterian Church and continued as the Protestant Cemetery until 1884.

Numerous visitors are buried there, those poor souls who came for their health but succumbed to illness. Three stories told by ghost-tour guides include the venerable Judge Stickney, the mischievous Erastus Nye, and the legendary John Manucy.

JUDGE JOHN B. STICKNEY

Arguably the most popular story is about Judge Stickney and his stolen gold teeth. Judge Stickney occupied a branch of a tree shadowing a monument resembling a bishop chesspiece on the east side of the cemetery. He was seen in that branch numerous times, and tour guides loved to point it out.

Although I can't be certain, I recall a time I thought I saw the good judge. I was talking to a group, and, as always, I watched faces for any signs of activity behind me. A young family stood before me, and even at dusk I could see their faces pale. They didn't point or talk, but it was enough for me to turn around and look. I saw a light on the branch where the judge usually sits. It disappeared as I looked at it, and I thought nothing more until 1999.

Hurricane Floyd hit Florida hard in September 1999. I was one of the evacuees. Upon return, my biggest concern was the Huguenot Cemetery, where Judge John B. Stickney's monument was situated. As I passed the cemetery on my way home, I saw that Judge Stickney's large tree limb had been severed from the tree by the strong winds. As quickly as possible I called Charles Tingley, senior research librarian of the St. Augustine Historical Society and president of the Friends of the Huguenot Cemetery. We approached the fallen branches with great trepidation but were pleasantly surprised to see that all the limbs and branches had fallen like gnarled fingers around the tombstones, guarding them from further damage. Who else but the good judge could have managed such a miraculous saving of precious stones? As it turned out, one stone was damaged when the branches were removed, and the judge's tree had to be cut down. I don't know where he sits today, but I am told he still wanders the small cemetery plot.

Here is the story as we tell it today. Judge Stickney was born in Lynn, Maine, in 1833. He moved to St. Augustine shortly after the Civil War. Now some say he was just another carpetbagger. But Judge Stickney archived considerable status not only in St. Augustine, but also in Florida as an attorney, judge, and the first chairman of the Republican Party. On a business trip to Washington, D.C., Judge Stickney became ill with fever.

As a matter of fact, he was not feeling well before he departed, but he left despite warnings. He was diagnosed as having typhoid fever and died within a few days after his arrival in the capital city. His body was transported back to St. Augustine by train and boat to be interred in the Huguenot Cemetery. Well-attended funeral services were held at Trinity Episcopal Church.

The judge's children were taken into custody by a friend and business associate, Judge John Long. Twenty-one years later, in 1903, the children requested that the body of their father be reinterred in Washington near Judge Long. A veteran grave digger, George Wells, opened the grave in September 1903. The body was found to be in a good state of preservation. A crowd of people gathered to watch the proceedings and, according to newspaper records, Wells stated that two men were seen handling the bones. He said they were under the influence of alcohol. Upon further examination he noted that several of Judge Stickney's gold-filled teeth were missing.

It has been said that the ghost of Judge Stickney appears to be wandering around the cemetery looking for something. Perhaps he is searching for his gold teeth. Or maybe he wants to find the person who took them. Then, again, maybe he just wants a good dentist.

ERASTUS NYE

Erastus Nye and his buddies John Lyman and John Gifford Hull are troublemakers. The three lie side by side in similar gravestones marking their deaths in January 1835. All were from northern cities. There was no accident reported at the time that would account for deaths so close in time. Cholera, however, had reached epidemic proportions in Georgia, the Carolinas, and Virginia. During the month of January, the local paper reassured everyone that "health in St. Augustine is excellent." Even then we were a tourist town, so it was not unusual to maintain an attractive image.[1]

Erastus and his pals must not be content with the circumstances of their deaths because they continue to tease tourists visiting the site, particularly those on ghost tours. As a guide on these nightly events and a friend of others conducting the evening walks, I have witnessed and heard of the deeds committed by these three. One of my several experiences directly involved mischievous Erastus, whose headstone has been recently restored by the Friends of the Huguenot Cemetery.

Tour guides carry lanterns for dramatic effect and efficiency. Guides can direct traffic with a well-lit lantern. The lantern I preferred was windproof. It was lit by lighter fluid, not candle wax, and carefully enclosed in glass. I thought about the secure lantern as I approached Erastus's tombstone site. I silently taunted the playful spirit to blow out my light. Within two feet of the cemetery, the hurricane-proof light went out. There was no wind, and I was carefully holding it upright. What happened is good story material, but I still puzzle over how that could have come to pass, except of course for Erastus's playful tricks. I did ask for it, though, didn't I?

The other incident involved a psychic I escorted around the cemetery with no stories explained in advance. We wandered the cemetery with the psychic absorbing the atmosphere. When we reached the graves of Erastus Nye, John Lyman, and John Gifford Hull, the woman tripped, falling against me. She clearly was agitated and said someone pushed her. I know she didn't stumble over anything on the ground, so I can only surmise that she was "pushed" by one of the boys. She wasn't hurt, and I don't know if I ever explained to her who the culprits were. It was up to her to figure it out.

The facts of these young men, and two others, remain important to our history. One of the five men significant to the history of St. Augustine died the same day as John Gifford Hull. Lieutenant Steven Tuttle (1797–1835) was a graduate of the U.S. Military Academy at West Point, with an engineering degree. He was responsible for the construction of the seawall on St. Augustine's bayfront. He was buried in the Huguenot Cemetery, but his remains were later moved to the National Cemetery in St. Augustine.

The fifth man was James Holt, who died in February 1835 at the age of thirty-seven. To summarize: the five men who died within a few weeks of each other in 1835 were Lyman, age twenty-six; Hull, twenty-seven; Nye, thirty-five; Tuttle, thirty-six; and Holt, thirty-seven. All were from northern states: Lyman, Northampton, Massachusetts; Hull, Poughkeepsie, New York; Nye, Onondaga, New York; Tuttle, Hanover, New Jersey; and Holt, New York City.

Of all of these men, the only one listed in history books is Stephen Tuttle. All of them now are being memorialized in our stories. Work in the Huguenot Cemetery continues to pay respect to these men interred in the burial grounds. By telling these stories we are putting symbolic flowers on the graves of five men who died young and alone.

DR. ANDERSON'S GREAT LOVE

The tombstone reads, "Her sun is gone down while it was yet day." Helen Porter Baldwin, nicknamed "Nellie," died at age sixteen and is buried in the Huguenot Cemetery with an elegant memorial seen by many tourists. Her death from typhoid fever was tragic not only to her family, but also to the man who loved her and shared letters with her while he was completing courses in the New York College of Physicians and Surgeons. That man is Dr. Andrew Anderson, and his contributions to the City of St. Augustine are extensive yet little recognized.

The death of Nellie was a life-changing experience for him. He received word of her demise in a letter from his mother, and his response was, "I feel as if, were it possible, I would never again fix my affections upon any-one, the end thereof is pain and sorrow."[2]

The tombstone for Nellie faces east, but ghost tours walking along the west fence see the back of it. Often a face appears on the west side, where a cross is carved into the stone. It is not unusual for people on the tours to see the face before the guide tells the story. Even when the guide does not tell the story, the face will appear to onlookers.

The legend of Nellie and Andrew Anderson's love for her supports the concept that ghost stories explain history. It is tragic that a sixteen-year-old died of typhoid fever, but sadder yet is the effect it had on a man who became important in the city. Dr. Anderson maintained his convictions that the little town of St. Augustine could become an impressive town.

Dr. Andrew Anderson became a friend and supporter of Henry Flagler. As a native to the city he could guide Flagler in his endeavors to change street names and lay bricks on streets and sidewalks previously layered with dirt or shell. He was a passionate worker in the town and strove to fill the void left by his father, whose ambition was to create a prosperous community. His education in northern schools gave him a different perspective from the town's southern natives. Despite his

An image continues to appear on the tombstone of Helen "Nellie" Porter Baldwin. Nellie's death made a significant impact on Andrew Anderson, who later became a physician, community leader, and friend of Henry M. Flagler. Photo courtesy of Tour St. Augustine.

Republican Party affiliations in a Democratic town, Anderson was elected city alderman in 1869 and 1875. He also served as a county commissioner and city mayor.[3]

His contributions include the magnificent marble lions at the end of the Bridge of Lions and the flagpole in front of the American Legion Post 37 building on the bayfront. His home, Markland, is a Greek Revival–style mansion now owned by Flagler College.

Dr. Anderson was a trustee of Memorial Presbyterian Church, the magnificent edifice built by Henry Flagler in memory of his daughter Jennie Louise. The Presbyterian Church in St. Augustine has owned the Huguenot Cemetery since 1832 and continues to maintain it. Dr. Anderson's daughter, Clarissa, remained a member of Memorial Presbyterian Church until her death in the 1990s. We hope Dr. Anderson would be pleased that the sun still shines on Nellie's grave and that she will be remembered.

LEGEND OR KLANSMAN

John Manucy's gravestone is a prominent marker at the front of the Huguenot Cemetery. Unfortunately, it has been damaged more than once. When upright, the stone rises behind a bordered plot marking the grave site.

During a day when the cemetery was open, I was approached by a woman who had been walking outside the cemetery fence the preceding night. She said she saw an image of a woman on the front of the stone. The impression showed up in a picture she took. We looked at the stone together and contemplated the possibility of a wife or lover. Since the stone was dedicated to Manucy by his wife, we felt it was her image that appeared on the stone.

It was an interesting question, but not a significant issue to pursue until the tombstone itself was damaged. During Hurricane Irma in September 2017, eight trees were blown down, including a huge century-old magnolia. The astonishing result of the devastation was that few tombstones were harmed. Tree limbs fell beside the stones with branches reaching around the memorials like arms protecting them from the

John Manucy's monument was the only stone blown down during the tornado that struck the Huguenot Cemetery during Hurricane Irma. Photo by Karen Harvey.

winds. It required months of clearing to determine the full extent of damage. As the fallen trees were removed and damages were assessed, it was clear the only stone harmed was John Manucy's. The fallen stone lay like a dead soldier on a battlefield. As clean-up work proceeded, a woman entered the cemetery, asking about the Manucy grave site. She was shown the plot, and she exclaimed, "That man was head of the Ku Klux Klan!" With this information came the need for further research.

It was common knowledge that Halstead "Hoss" Manucy was the KKK leader in the 1960s. John Manucy died in 1879. The tombstone clearly reads "age 59 years, 9 months and 27 days."

Could he have been a Klan member? The first Klan was established by the Democratic Party after the Civil War during the end of the Reconstruction era, 1876–77. It is possible that John Manucy participated in the movement, and it is more than possible that Hoss Manucy knew of his ancestor's activity a full century before he became the infamous Klan leader.

Research shows that John Manucy was a gunsmith married to a young woman named Dionicia. She was only nineteen years of age when she married a thirty-two-year-old man. The 1870 census records indicate they had six children.

The dedicated wife of John inscribed the stone "To my husband" with the dates of birth and death. She must have loved the man to go to that effort to place a tombstone in his honor.

We will never know whose image was seen on the stone. Nor will we ever be sure whether he was part of the Ku Klux Klan. What we do know is that his tombstone was the only one in the cemetery damaged during Hurricane Irma in September 2017. All of the other stones remain untouched. For example, the stone of Rev. Wilbur Nields was an inch away from the fallen magnolia tree. No tree toppled the Manucy stone; it simply fell. Was it because of past actions? We cannot say.

The Manucy name remains significant in St. Augustine. Albert Manucy (1910–1997) is remembered by historians as the author of *Sixteenth-Century St. Augustine: The People and Their Homes*. Manucy received a master's degree in history from the University of Florida in 1934 and studied Spanish architecture in Spain on a Fulbright Scholarship. He worked for the

A bright orb appears in a photo taken in the Huguenot Cemetery. Orbs are unusual appearances. The phenomenon is considered to be an organized pattern of energy captured on film in places of supernatural activity. Photo courtesy of Tour St. Augustine.

National Park Service and served as the official historian of the Castillo de San Marcos, across the street from the Huguenot Cemetery. He and all of the Manucy descendants trace their lineage to Josef Manucy, one of the original Minorcan immigrants of the New Smyrna plantation who escaped indentured servitude and walked to St. Augustine in 1777 to begin a new life in the city that had been Spanish but was occupied by the British when they arrived.

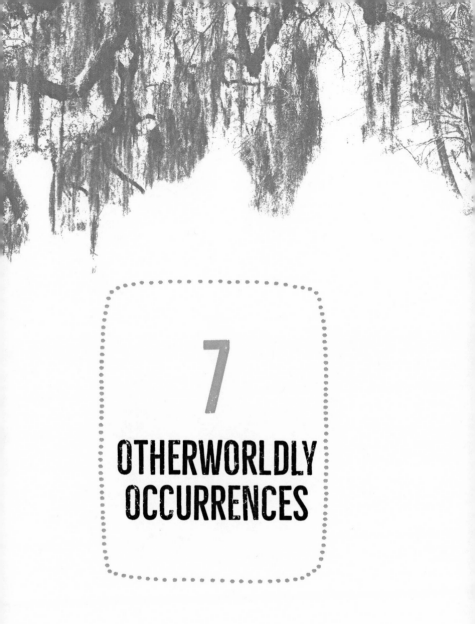

7

OTHERWORLDLY OCCURRENCES

FAY

No one liked Fay before she died, and no one liked her after her demise. Fay was so obnoxious the owners of the building on the corner of Cuna and Spanish streets restricted the ghost-tour guides from standing in front of the building, although her story was a popular one. She was driving people away from the café establishment after her death.

Fay remains one of the most active spirits in town, with her presence felt as detestable by all who have encountered her. According to legend, Fay was an angry and outspoken woman who did little upkeep on her house. When the stairs to her second floor deteriorated, she hired a carpenter to repair them. She did not approve of the work done by the workman and told him with an acerbic tongue to leave her house. The carpenter left, and shortly afterward Fay fell to her death on the staircase she had ruled unfit. No one knows if the staircase was unsafe, but Fay died from the fall, and her body was not found for several days.

For years the image of a scowling woman was seen in a window of the house. Tour guide Candace Fleming saw her more than once and often asked the groups she was leading if they could see her. Hands were raised in acknowledgment of seeing the vision. Of course, we can all see images we are told to see, but I believe Fay's appearances outnumbered the odds. It is sad that no one liked the old lady, and her story is not one that is told to remember a person of goodwill. But her memory lives on with all the embellishments provided by the storytellers.

NATIONAL CEMETERY COFFIN

Occasionally a new story surfaces that takes on a life of its own. I was contacted by Jim Kelly, who said he lived by the St. Augustine National Cemetery and had an experience he wanted to share with me. I expected he had seen spiritual activity in the burial ground, but that was not the case. His story led to further research and left unanswered questions.

The front door of Jim's house faces the south wall of the National Cemetery. He revealed that he had looked out the window one day and saw the image of a man sitting in a chair on his porch. He described the figure as a man wearing a "red coat, white shirt, pantaloons and boots." A red coat usually means British, but the Spanish wore red vests under their blue coats and were often seen around the Castillo de San Marcos in the red garment when it was too hot to wear the heavy woolen blue coat. The image could have been any number of people, but Jim remains certain it was a military man he saw.

The cemetery beside St. Francis Barracks on Marine Street was first used for interments in 1828. It was a significant burial ground for soldiers and their families stationed in St. Augustine, particularly those involved in the Seminole Indian Wars.

In August 2007 an excavation took place on the corner of Charlotte and San Salvador streets. The project was consistent with the city policy of requiring an archaeologist to excavate before any major construction work started. The city was laying a new water line, and Carl Halbirt, the archaeologist, sifted through dirt while construction workers waited. While it was known that the southern end of the walled city was in the area of San Salvador Street, the chance of finding further evidence of the boundary was exciting to the archaeologists. Halbirt had already located a 1720s well at 1 San Salvador Street. What they found this time exceeded expectations. It was a water system that city officials dubbed "the first public works project in the country."[1]

With all the excitement going on in front of Jim Kelly's house, the discovery of a coffin with bones was more than anyone had anticipated. The remains were of a man who might have been of Native American heritage. According the archaeological findings, the body was of someone who was strong and in good shape. A medical examiner wrote, "The bones were quite robust, with notable muscle markings." There was no evidence of a homicide or death by accident. Carl Halbirt felt the man had been buried sometime between the 1820s and the construction of the wall in the 1850s. He could perhaps have been a participant in the Seminole Indian Wars. He was buried with dignity, his arms folded over his chest, "his head to the east, his feet to the west." The conclusion from the Human Identification Laboratory of the University of Florida was that this was "a male about forty years of age who led a physically active life. The individual may be of Native American ethnicity, but this is by no means certain."[2]

We may never know the identity of the individual or why he was buried outside the cemetery wall. Jim Kelly knows he saw a vision of a man on his porch and believes it was the man found buried in front of his house. He has not seen the vision since the discovery of the coffin and suggested now the soul of the deceased is at peace. Perhaps it is, but the story remains with unanswered questions. Who was he, and why was he buried outside the cemetery? Perhaps we will know some day. His remains are in place where he was buried, and we all hope he does rest in peace.

DEATH BY FIRE: A TRIBUTE TO RUTH

Ripley's Believe It or Not! Museum contains secrets beyond the bizarre exhibits. The first Ripley's Museum in the world is located in St. Augustine. The exhibits are housed in a building that was once Warden Castle, the winter home of William Grey Warden, a partner in Standard Oil with John D. Rockefeller and Henry Morrison Flagler.

In 1941, after the last Warden heir died, the building was sold to Norton Baskin. Baskin was a hotelier and the husband of Pulitzer Prize–winner Marjorie Kinnan Rawlings, who won her honor for *The Yearling*. Baskin had a penthouse available in Castle Warden Hotel for his wife when she was in town. At the time of the incident, the suite was occupied by Marjorie's friend Ruth Pickering, age forty-nine. The disaster occurred at 11 a.m. Sunday, April 23, 1944, and it was reported that many of the hotel guests were either at church or at the beach.[3]

Below the suite was a room occupied by Betty Neville Richeson, a young woman in her twenties. Betty had just arrived from Jacksonville. When the fire started in her room, she called for the bellboy, but apparently the fire had already spread to the hall and she could not escape. It extended upward to the penthouse. Screams were heard from the windows, but rescuers were too late to save the women. Both were found dead of smoke inhalation in their bathrooms. It appeared they tried to save themselves from asphyxiation by covering their heads with wet towels.

The significance of this story is that many people see a woman standing at an upper window in Ripley's. The story has been told by employees and numerous people who travel West Castillo Drive toward the entrance to the museum. People who are sensitive to spiritual activity have difficulty entering the section of the museum near Betty Richeson's room. It is now an exhibit room, and no one could make the association unless told about the fire.

Most significant is a letter written by Marjorie Kinnan Rawlings to *St. Augustine Record* columnist Langston Moffet and printed in the paper on April 30, 1944. Marjorie Rawlings said about her friend, Ruth Pickering:

> "She hid her light under a bushel." Through this coincidence of thought, I was struck with two elements in Ruth's nature; her humility and her luminosity.
>
> Out of this self-effacing but ineffaceable brightness some of us became aware of a phenomenon, which was the same quality in "our town," rising in answer, like one light signaling to another, Goodness and kindness are infectious, as unfortunately is hate also. So many of us were struck by your making. In your sincere and beautiful tribute, the key point that she was totally without malice, and she had been incapable of an unkind word or thought.[4]

The beautiful tribute continues. Although we know less about Betty, who died below Ruth's hotel room, we know they both suffered a tragic death together.

It is apparent by their spiritual appearances that one or both want to be remembered. That really is not necessary. Thousands of visitors pass by an exhibit with a plaque displaying their names. Although it is doubtful that visitors give much thought to it, it is seen every day by hundreds of tourists.

Reading Marjorie Kinnan Rawlings's words, we know that Ruth should be remembered as a dear friend, and by association, so should Betty. Ripley's Museum will keep the memories alive far longer than a gravestone would.

CONCLUSION

THE DIVERSE CULTURAL HISTORY of St. Augustine is reflected in the ghost stories recounted here. When people experience an unusual occurrence, they may not want to talk about it. That seemed to be the case in St. Augustine for many years. Now, however, the stories draw crowds to nightly tours. This is a big attraction for St. Augustine and is beneficial as long as the stories continue to provide historic information.

Naturally the tours have to be entertaining, but we are also teaching through telling the stories. The stories span several centuries and reflect the cultural heritage of the Ancient City. So many people are remembered daily by telling these tales, and that is an appealing aspect of repeating the stories. We all can benefit from these interactions of storytelling and history.

ACKNOWLEDGMENTS

I am grateful to everyone who has contributed family tales and factual information to this endeavor. It is not surprising that many stories take place in the two historic cemeteries in the historic neighborhoods of St. Augustine. One is the Tolomato Cemetery, 16 Cordova Street, the western boundary of the walled city.

Elizabeth Duran Gessner, president of the Tolomato Cemetery Preservation Association, has guided me through the process of understanding all the changes that have taken place in recent years. Her tours, in period clothing, are remarkable. Margo Pope has been exceptionally helpful in understanding the background of the stories about the Tolomato Cemetery. Margo, a native of St. Augustine and a career newspaper reporter and editor, shared information that is held in her memory and her knowledge of source documentation.

Though not as old as Tolomato, the Huguenot Cemetery, north of the City Gate, is also a popular place for ghost tours.

For historic information not readily available, I rely on Charles Tingley at the St. Augustine Historical Society Research Library and president of the Friends of the Huguenot Cemetery. Charles claims he does not believe in ghosts but will provide any documentation I request. Questions always lead to new material and more answers for interpreting our past.

Robert Smith has helped by cleaning and interpreting the writing on tombstones in the Huguenot Cemetery and discovering family ties with other cemeteries. He has dedicated his time to maintaining the burial ground and reading my stories related to the history.

The staff at Tour St. Augustine has been most supportive. It was Sandy Craig who founded Tour St. Augustine and originated the ghost tours. As a heritage native she strongly believed in protecting our heritage. Thank you to Alan Hudson and Cathy Hatton for supplying updated information and pictures.

My Minorcan friends Michelle Reyna and Carol Lopez Bradshaw provided background information that helped me understand the Minorcan culture. Ann Browning Masters's literary contribution gives credence to the Minorcan story.

Fictitious names are used in the printed stories when individuals prefer not to be identified. When a full name appears, it is considered part of the history of St. Augustine.

There are few people who have followed my writing career more closely than my friend Roberta "Sherlock" Butler, who proofreads like a sleuth. I thank her for her meticulous attention to detail and her questioning mind. She has also been an important part of preserving the history of the Huguenot Cemetery included as a section in this book. I also thank my new friend Cindi Smith for her support and interest in our past.

The history of the Ancient City must always be preserved, and it takes a community to do that.

NOTES

INTRODUCTION

1. A quote from a review of Dickey's book was printed in the *St. Augustine Record* in an October 29, 2017, review.

CHAPTER 1. COLONIAL SPANISH TALES: 1565–1821

1. Cathy Hatton, training manager, Ghost Tours and City Walks, Tour St. Augustine.
2. Letter dated October 21, 1809, from Governor Enrique White to Father O'Reilly, in Cathedral Parish Records.
3. Library of Congress HABS FLA-130. NRHP 71001014. Information is available in the St. Augustine Historical Society Research Library.
4. National Park Service Interpretive Series: "Artillery Through the Ages: A Short Illustrated History of Cannon, Emphasizing Types Used in America."
5. Pirates and Privateers: The History of Maritime Piracy, www.cindyvallar .com/StAugustine.html.

CHAPTER 3. INTO TERRITORIAL DAYS

1. Gannon, *The Cross in the Sand*, 164–89.
2. Dr. Michael Gannon left the priesthood in 1976 to become an educator at the University of Florida and an author of many books. He died in April 2017.

3. Information by Elizabeth Duran Gessner can be read on the Tolomato Cemetery website.

Chapter 4. Statehood

1. Geoff Dobson, Historic City Memories: Two mules for widow Abbott, www.historiccity.com.

Chapter 6. Huguenot Cemetery

1. *Florida Herald,* January 1835.
2. Graham, *The Awakening of St. Augustine,* 83.
3. Harvey, *St. Augustine and St. Johns County: A Pictorial History,* 92.

Chapter 7. Otherworldly Occurrences

1. *St. Augustine Record,* April 24, 1944.
2. *St. Augustine Record,* April 30, 1944.
3. St. *Augustine Record,* August 7 and 24, 2007.
4. David Z. C. Hines, M.A., C. A. Pound Human Identification Laboratory, University of Florida, September 4, 2007.

BIBLIOGRAPHY

Beeson, Kenneth H., Jr. *Fromajadas and Indigo*. Charleston, S.C.: History Press, 2006.

Dickey, Colin. *Ghostland and American History in Haunted Places*. New York: Penguin Books, 2016.

Gannon, Michael V. *The Cross in the Sand*. Gainesville: University of Florida Press, 1965, 1967.

Graham, Thomas. *The Awakening of St. Augustine: The Anderson Family and the Oldest City: 1821–1924*. St. Augustine: St. Augustine Historical Society, 1978.

Griffin, Patricia C. *Mullet on the Beach: The Minorcans of Florida (1768–1788)*. Jacksonville: University of North Florida Press, 1991.

Harvey, Karen. *Daring Daughters: St. Augustine's Feisty Females 1565–2000*. Virginia Beach, Va.: Donning Co., 2002.

———. *Oldest Ghosts: St. Augustine Haunts*. Sarasota, Fla.: Pineapple Press, 2000.

———. *St. Augustine and St. Johns County: A Pictorial History*. Virginia Beach, Va.: Donning Co., 1980.

Hughes, Nathaniel Cheairs, Jr. *General William J. Hardee: Old Reliable*. Baton Rouge: Louisiana State University Press, 1965.

Masters, Ann Browning. *Floridanos, Menorcans, Cattle-Whip Crackers: Poetry of St. Augustine*. Cocoa: Florida Historical Society Press, 2015.

Moore, Gregory A. *Sacred Ground: The Military Cemetery at St. Augustine*. St. Augustine: Florida National Guard Foundation, 2013.

Randall, Elizabeth. *Haunted St. Augustine and St. Johns County*. Charleston, S.C.: History Press, 2013.

Stavley, John F. *Ghosts and Gravestones in St. Augustine, Florida*. St. Augustine: Historic Tours of America, 2004.

Tebeau, Charlton W., and William Marina. *A History of Florida*. 3rd ed. Coral Gables: University of Miami Press, 1999.

Vallar, Cindy, ed. *The Pirates of San Agustín*. www.cindyvallar.com/StAugustine.html.

KAREN HARVEY has been writing about St. Augustine's history since arriving in the city in 1978. Her books reflect various aspects of the town's culture, including ghost tales. She was working as arts-and-entertainment editor at the *St. Augustine Record* when she was approached by the news editor, who asked why St. Augustine didn't have any ghost stories. The question led to a search for stories of paranormal activity or simply strange occurrences. The ghost stories collected by Harvey and published by the *Record* were later used as the basis for the first ghost tours in the Oldest City.

Harvey spent several years conducting tours and knows the tales reflecting the city's history. She continues to work and live in the Ancient City and devotes much of her time to recording its history. Her first book, *St. Augustine and St. Johns County: A Pictorial History,* is in its ninth printing since its first publication in 1980. *Daring Daughters: St. Augustine's Feisty Females 1565–2000* contains stories about women often overlooked in history. Two volumes of *Legends and Tales* tell stories as people told them to Harvey.

Her most recent publication, *St. Augustine Enters the Twenty-First Century,* updates the first pictorial book by pointing out growth from 1980 to 2010. In 2010 it won the Florida Writers Association Royal Palm Literary Award for Best Nonfiction Book.

Harvey also has written anniversary-celebration books for Flagler Hospital and Memorial Presbyterian Church. Her play, *Conquest and Colonization,* ran for five spring seasons at the St. Augustine Amphitheater. She has written museum copy for the St. Photios Greek Orthodox National Shrine and the St. Augustine Lighthouse and Museum.